Pets with Tourette's

**Mike Lepine &
Mark Leigh**

summersdale

PETS WITH TOURETTE'S

Summersdale Publishers Ltd
46 West Street
Chichester
West Sussex
PO19 1RP
UK

www.summersdale.com

Printed and bound by MS-Printing.

ISBN: 1-84024-610-3

ISBN 13: 978-1-84024-610-0

For Zippy, the rudest cat in the history of cats

Thank yous

The authors would like to thank the following people for their assistance and tolerance: Philippa Hatton-Lepine, Gage Hatton-Lepine, Rob Shreeve, Debbie Leigh, Polly & Barney Leigh (kids – don't ever read this book) and Robert Day – who wanted to be mentioned in a tasteful and sophisticated work of literature.

Meet the authors

Mike Lepine and Mark Leigh have had over thirty humour/trivia books published including three number one best-sellers. Celebrities they have worked with include Adrian Edmondson, Julian Clary, Des Lynam, Jeremy Beadle, Roy Chubby Brown, Chris Tarrant and Rolf Harris.

They have also written and developed numerous TV programmes and recently completed their first comedy film screenplay (it's really funny and they are eagerly awaiting a top Hollywood movie agent or studio exec to contact them).

www.summersdale.com